REBECCA HORN
BUSTER'S BEDROOM

a filmbook

Director of Photography SVEN NYKVIST
Script REBECCA HORN & MARTIN MOSEBACH
based on a story by REBECCA HORN

PARKETT PUBLISHERS   Zürich – Frankfurt – New York

At the artist's discretion,
some images in this edition of
Buster's Bedroom appear reversed.

Parkett Publishers Ltd., Quellenstr. 27, CH-8005 Zurich
636 Broadway, New York, N.Y. 10012
Schweizerstr. 77, 6000 Frankfurt/M 70.

ISBN 3-907509-13-7 First Edition

Billing and Cooing, Fluttering and Budding

BICE CURIGER

In Rebecca Horn's films, the action is always confined to a particular interior space: In EINTÄNZER (1978), a studio; in LA FERDINANDA – EINE SONATA FÜR EINE MEDICI-VILLA (1981), a building; and now, in BUSTER'S BEDROOM, "Nirvana House", a sanatorium. The films examine the tension in the demarcation between "inside" and "outside"; the protective skins or shells of the conspicuously sensitive inhabitants of the dwellings thus described.

The interiors mirror the inner lives of their inhabitants, and in BUSTER'S BEDROOM, we find ourselves being lured into complicity with the protagonists. What a pleasure it is to watch the figures moving before us baring their souls with shameless abandon! The spaces are suffused with an intimacy in which the absent is undeniably present, as in the detached proximity of Buster Keaton. The main activities of the protagonists are, however, concealment and deception. Their curious predilection for special clothing, body shells, uniforms, and even straitjackets is obvious. Diana Daniels wears only shocking red and O'Connor a white doctor's coat, although we cannot be sure whether it is authentic – it belonged to the deceased head physician – or fake – since it has been illegally but necessarily appropriated. The nurses, who are, in fact, actresses, are urged to wear their uniforms (or, in case of emergencies, at *least* their caps!) at all times to distinguish them from the patients. And Mr. Warlock's apparel is reminiscent of a bumblebee.

Bustling earnestness characterizes life in this strange clinic. The inhabitants are all fully aware that their activities are governed by a complex system of self-imposed rules and regulations and we, the spectators, are soon cunningly initiated as conspirators. It is this modicum of extra knowledge that gives the film its basic note of irony as it unfolds in sequences of arabesque play, from cheerful nonchalance to bitterly serious constructions.

We experience the inmates' play at its most dramatic in their organizing of Seraphina Tannenbaum's sham love affair with the sham soldier, Maurice, or in Mr. Warlock's agitated response to Micha's questions about Buster Keaton – "Oh, no names! No names! … You see, if you say a name and I say no, that's the end of that. No more conversation. Tragic!"

The group all seem to take the grotesquely ludicrous implications of their play in their stride. This indifference, coupled with their blatantly unscrupulous behavior, testifies to the dramatic necessity that underlies the surface playfulness of these hypersensitive souls. "Nirvana is the transcendence of all factors that determine the burden of being, the extinction of the lust for life and the delusion of perceiving reality in being" *(Meyers Großes Taschen Lexikon)*. It is not quite certain whether the residents of the clinic in BUSTER'S BEDROOM are seeking to attain the ideal state of Nirvana as described here or whether, once again, this idea is rooted in the realm of ironic deception. However one thing is certain: in Buster's Nirvana, elaborate though futile activity is the order of the day, not to repress the energies inherent in the "lust for life", but to stimulate, kindle and incite them with concentrated purpose.

"You feel like a volcano inside today", says O'Connor to Diana Daniels, who is incensed by Micha's intrusion into the clinic. Diana retorts, "She's spiritually immature! The young have no power of concentration. She'd be absolutely hopeless at immobility training." Perseverance, discipline and devotion to ritual mark the attitude of a genuine inmate of Nirvana House. Actually there are no restrictions except against leaving the protective confines of the institutional and regulative cocoon. Objectively, the greatest danger lurks in the form of the investigative Winterbottom Foundation, also known as the "Ethics Committee" which, as the name implies, means certain death to the billing and cooing and fluttering and budding of carnal life in Nirvana House.

In 1985 Rebecca Horn created an object titled THERMOMETRE D'AMOUR which integrates twenty-one words as a kind of calibrated scale of love, ranging from "solitude" to "disintegration" with such intermediate stages as "vulnerability", "hovering" and "madness". Often the inmates of Nirvana House seem to be endowed with a substantial but unfathomable reservoir of such experiences and secrets. Filmmakers have taken to drowning audiences in a deluge of explanations for the social and psychological makeup of their screen characters. No such fetish is made in Rebecca Horn's films. We are left to make our own observations. We are challenged to activate our own eroticizing perceptions and our perhaps dormant awareness of abysses and the necessary lifesaving grips to empathize with the spectacularly imaginative acrobatics of the exotic creatures in BUSTER'S BEDROOM.

At times, events take such a turn that Nirvana House seems like a spluttering engine trying to run on the wrong fuel. In fact much of the film is contingent upon mechanics. The inmates are enamored of mechanical devices, artificial limbs, antennae: Mr. Warlock with his giant palm frond duster; Diana Daniels in her wheelchair to which she is voluntarily confined; Lenny Silver cherishes his piano as much for its mechanicity as for the music it produces; they all make use of the binoculars, testifying once again to their love of prosthetic devices.

Mechanisms serve to absorb and transmit vibrations. They are useful in a mysterious, indirect, sophisticating fashion because they do not resort to high technology but rather entail transparent and fragile systems. Often second and third parties are in control of the mechanical operations that affect someone else. Either the doctor or one of the nurses has to activate the mechanical arm that raises the whisky glass, attached to Diana Daniels' wheelchair, to her lips; O'Connor makes summary use of the elevator button to take a brief respite from Diana; and the "genuine" doctor does not even administer his own morphine. It is as if they are trying to plumb the depths of Mr. Warlock's comments about the unconscious Micha – "She's so exquisitely defenceless."

Nirvana House is a receptacle, a large receptacle for a variety of smaller ones all conceived to shelter vulnerable creatures: boxes, glass terrariums for snakes, an aviary, a refrigerator for butterflies; an elevator and an ambulance are less obvious containers camouflaged as utilitarian vehicles.

The interacting mechanics of the horizontal and the vertical are compounded with other forces to produce foci of nervous activity that arise out of waves of overlapping motion. The swimming pool is a settling pond for savage emotions not only by appearance; it is here in the moment of greatest uproar that Diana Daniels finds her final resting place.

The film begins and ends outside Nirvana House. It opens with Micha driving through the desert and closes as she escapes with Joe into the breakers, swimming away to elude the clutches of O'Connor and his consorts.

In the searing heat of the desert, Micha, driving blindfold down the highway, embodies a dangerous lust for adventure: the death wish. Having waived the use of one of her senses with her blue blindfold (the color of Romanticism) in order to look inwards and enhance the coveted thrill, she demonstrates her affinity with the residents of Nirvana House. Once there, she is immediately subjected to a purgatory of tests, all of which she passes with Keatonesque verve. In the process she is encouraged to discover that the powers of mental discipline can be as great as those of poison, drugs and fire. Restrained in a straitjacket she, the intruder, effects a brilliant escape and succeeds in playing the same tune better than O'Connor and Diana Daniels, who have done nothing but talk about their lifelong "project".

As viewers, we are reminded now and again that the Latin word for room is *camera,* and that we are sitting in a darkened space where we have surrendered ourselves to a phenomenon that rests on the interdependence of mechanics and imagination: the moving picture.

Translation from the German: Catherine Schelbert

MUSIC.

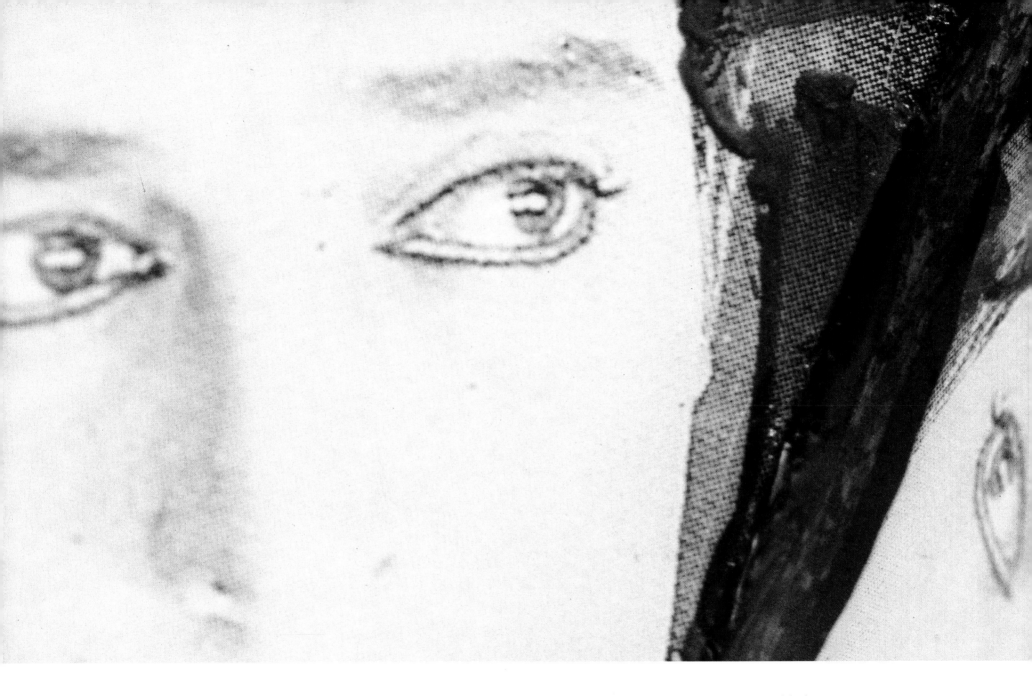

MUSIC.

MICHA's VOICE
You have such beautiful eyes.
You never laugh
Why do you always seek danger?
Is it to have a reason to escape?
You are not afraid at all.
In the back of your mind maybe you are.

You don't need help.
You would run away from it anyway!
Keep to yourself.
There's nothing left to lose.
Take me to the other side of the ocean
You can't get rid of me.
I'm part of you.

MUSIC.

Micha, a young girl, is driving blindfold down an endless, straight road in the Californian desert, playing a kind of blindman's bluff, trying to exorcise her fear of death. An oncoming truck blows its horn; the two vehicles just miss each other.
A motorcyclist, who has just witnessed the narrow escape, overtakes her.

GUY ON A MOTORBIKE What's wrong with you?
Get the fuck off the road!

LOS ANGELES. Micha arrives at the studio of her father's old girlfriend.

MICHA Hi!

JANE Micha! What are you doing here! You're supposed to be at your father's funeral in New York!

MICHA Didn't you get my letter? It was two weeks ago.

JANE Oh, we don't open our mail anymore. Micha, this is Steve. Steve, this is Micha… How are you? Still in love with Buster Keaton, I see.

MICHA Yeah.

JANE You know where the keys are. Stay as long as you like!

MICHA Thank you.

JANE You are at home.

MICHA So when will you be back?

JANE When we split up. Steve! Get in the car! 'Bye!

They roar off without looking back, leaving the bemused Micha alone in the parking lot.

JANE'S STUDIO. Micha is on the telephone. On TV, Buster Keaton is performing in Steamboat Bill Jr. Micha calls Mrs. Noah, an old friend of Buster Keaton.

MICHA Mrs. Noah? Is this Mrs. Noah? My name is Micha Morgan. A friend of mine gave me your number. She said that you knew Buster Keaton.

MRS. NOAH Keaton! That old bum!
MICHA I wonder if we could meet?

MRS. NOAH Keaton is dead, honey. I lost track of him a long time ago.

MICHA You knew him pretty well though, didn't you?

MRS. NOAH Well, we used to get drunk together.
MICHA Then you were close?

MRS. NOAH Oh yes darling, we were. Except that they took him off and put him in a straitjacket. But he was able to free himself and came back. It was one of those wild flirtations, until he upped and married this nurse.

MICHA He probably did it to keep himself out of hospitals.

MRS. NOAH You have to be joking honey! That battleaxe put him in Nirvana House.

MICHA That doesn't sound like a hospital, "Nirvana House." Does it still exist?
MRS. NOAH Sure! Nirvana House, south of Santa Barbara. Couldn't think of a better place myself

for the few genius artists in this town!
Micha absentmindedly spears a raspberry with a fork, leaving it on the plate. A faint rustling sound interrupts the silence. On the other side of the room

a chameleon slowly changes color to bright raspberry red.

NIRVANA HOUSE. Mr. Warlock, a patient at Nirvana House, is playing at being "bee", buzzing and pollinating the lone palm tree in front of the building.

KITCHEN, NIRVANA HOUSE.
DR. JACOBY What's keeping you for Christ's sake? Hurry up!

NURSE FOWLER It's always the same. I can't find anything in this goddamned refrigerator. O'Connor has filled it all up with his junk.

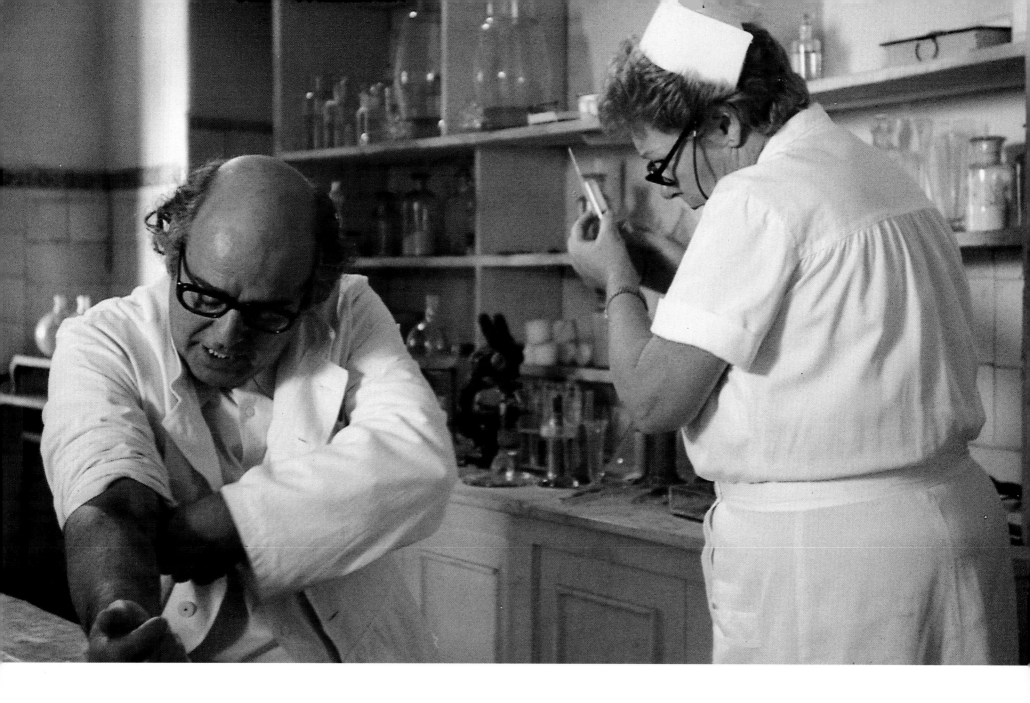

DR. JACOBY This goddamned sanatorium is totally fucked up. We can't even afford a new 'fridge!

NURSE FOWLER Because the money goes you know where!

DR. JACOBY That's my business ... cut the crap and give me the shot.

The nurse gives him a shot. Instantly the doctor's face pales, shock distorts his features. He is dead.

SOUTH AMERICAN BAR, LOS ANGELES. The bar is nearly empty. A waiter is putting chairs up on the tables. Music.

On the dance floor, a pale five year old girl is playing with a wooden top which she spins with a little whip. The sound of the whip striking the top mingles with a monotonous, hammering rhythm.

Micha is sitting alone at a table. She spreads out the fingers of her left hand sheathed in a fine black leather glove. In her right hand she holds an open pocket knife with which she stabs relentlessly at the spaces between each finger.

The waiter, a young Spanish-looking man with a moustache, approaches her hesitantly.
JOE I could never do that.
MICHA It's nothing but concentration. In this moment I am the knife *and* the space between my fingers.
JOE Do you believe in love at first sight?
MICHA Oh no!

Micha gets up to leave. Joe looks disappointedly after her.

NIRVANA HOUSE. Snake room in the basement of Nirvana House. O'Connor is feeding his snakes.

DIANA DANIELS Sometimes I feel I should just give up.

O'CONNOR Don't, Diana.

DIANA DANIELS Isn't it time for breakfast?

O'CONNOR After I give them theirs.

DIANA DANIELS You care more for them than you do for me ... I can't seem to just switch off the way they do.

O'CONNOR Do you want to learn from them or not, Diana?

DIANA DANIELS Why else do you think I'd be sitting in this wheelchair so obediently? ... God, I'm getting stiff!

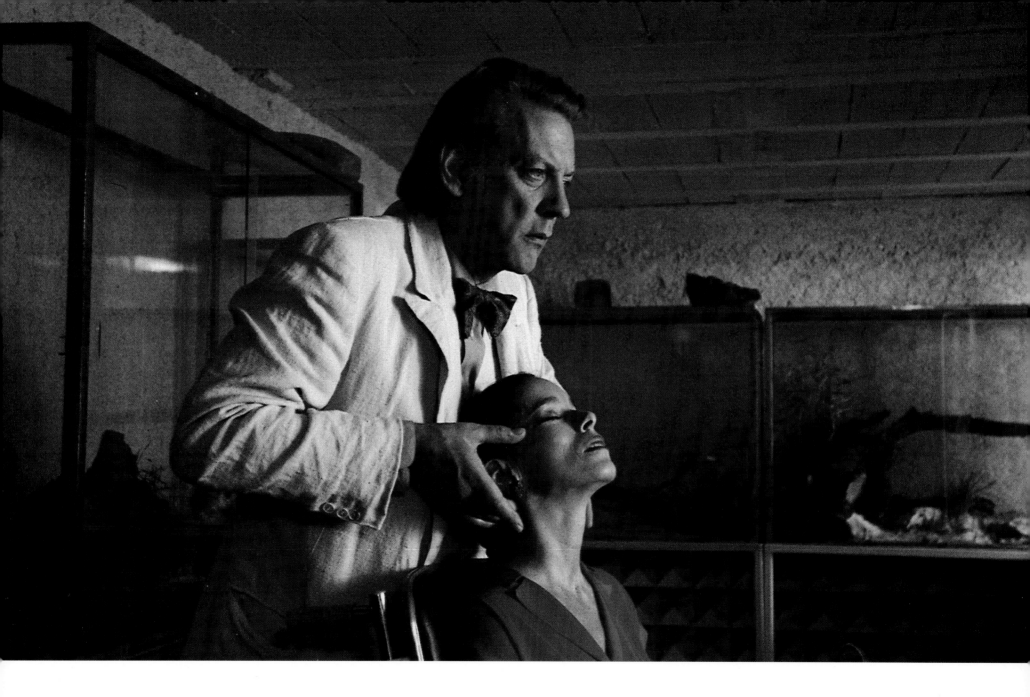

O'CONNOR And the snake gets rigid. That's its secret.
DIANA DANIELS O'Connor, give me a massage.
O'CONNOR Only if you promise not to move a muscle.

DIANA DANIELS I promise ... There's drama rampant in my body, O'Connor. But if I stay still for long enough I will shoot from this wheelchair like sprung steel, won't I?
O'CONNOR I swear it. I've been thinking this

problem through for years, that is, the secret of the snake's energy.

MAIN ROOM. The patients of Nirvana House are having their first meeting since Dr. Jacoby's death.

JAMES I'm afraid I have some disturbing news for all of us... As you know, Nurse Fowler is a bit short-sighted. And it was crazy of Dr. Jacoby to keep his morphine in the same 'fridge as Mr. O'Connor's snake venom. Why couldn't he ever listen to me?

SERAFINA He is not going to try and use my 'fridge again. If my butterflies are disturbed every time the doctor needs his concoction, they will go beserk!

JAMES They shall not be, Madam. I don't know exactly what happened. Nurse Fowler has disappeared screaming into the desert with her secret and Dr. Jacoby is dead and has no further need of morphine.

JAMES I can only assume that he was a victim of

mistaken identity.

MR. WARLOCK Do you mean to say that we have been abandoned by science?

JAMES I'm afraid so, sir! There is nothing much to cheer about ladies and gentlemen. The Ethics Committee of the Winterbottom Foundation arrives today. If they don't find their establishment running well, they'll close it down.

MR. WARLOCK Oh, we just don't have a doctor!

LENNY SILVER It's impossible! My work can't be interrupted!

DIANA DANIELS And I haven't been in training for fourteen years for this to happen now!

LENNY SILVER What is a doctor?

SERAFINA A white coat...

MR. WARLOCK A stethoscope...

DIANA DANIELS A signature...

LENNY SILVER Doesn't anybody understand

what I'm getting at? It's right in front of you! Somebody just has to do it!

O'Connor enters the room.

MR. WARLOCK Look, it's Doctor O'Connor!

JAMES Mr. O'Connor, that research you did with those tribes up the Amazon somewhere... could that work here? You told us, didn't you, that you'd cured them of all our civilized diseases?

O'CONNOR No, no James, they cured *me* of all civilized diseases... but I don't think that their methodology would be accepted here. I'm working on the field trials now.

MR. WARLOCK O'Connor, I meant what I said just now. Dr. Jacoby has abandoned us and we need a replacement. You have credibility. Use it!

O'CONNOR But I'm a scholar! I can't make diagnoses. I can't write prescriptions.
JAMES But we'd all pitch in.
O'CONNOR I'm in the middle of such wonderful progress with Mrs. Daniels. I feel that I am on the edge of an earth-shattering discovery.
DIANA DANIELS You're on the edge of a catastrophe, if reputable doctors are allowed back here.
LENNY SILVER They will take away my piano. O'Connor, they will take away your snakes. Serafina, your butterflies!
O'CONNOR You leave me no choice. I accept. But there are conditions: you must address me as Doctor O'Connor, but the role will be purely

symbolic. There will be no consulting hours. JAMES No problem, Doctor. Nobody must leave the clinic. If the number of patients falls below four, the Foundation has the right to close

Nirvana House.
O'CONNOR So, absolutely yes, I must insist that no one leaves my clinic. And I need your word of honor on that. Mr Silver? ... Mr Warlock? ...

Mrs. Tannenbaum? ... Mrs. Daniels?
In her enthusiasm, Diana starts from her wheelchair.
O'CONNOR ... Don't move Diana! ... Fourteen years ... good grief ...

OFFICE. MR. WARLOCK Well, Nurse Fowler was awful. Now that she's gone we have an unique opportunity.

JAMES (on the 'phone) Yes, is this the Burbank Emergency Nursing Service? I'd like a replacement for Nurse Fowler...

MR. WARLOCK Excuse me, James, you don't really appreciate what's at stake ... Hello, this is Nirvana House ... yes, the vicepresident of the board of directors. We're looking for a nurse, maybe even two ... Caps are important ... and empathy ... oh, young ladies ... musical if possible ... immediately!

JAMES Why did you request young ladies, sir?

MR. WARLOCK Oh, I have this longing for something completely out of the ordinary ... soft blonde hair like pollen from a flower ...

JAMES Yes, how about a couple of sailors? We are desperate ... They're all at sea? ... April?

THE GARDENS AT NIRVANA HOUSE.
JAMES You look very convincing...
O'CONNOR Convincing as what?
JAMES As a doctor, of course.
O'CONNOR Well then, say it!

JAMES Oh dear me! I only wanted you, Doctor O'Connor, to know that you look like a doctor.
O'CONNOR Good. And do you know what you look like, James.
JAMES No ... Doctor.

O'CONNOR Good. I don't think you would be able to live with my diagnosis.
Micha walks up the driveway looking inquisitively towards Nirvana House. She takes out her camera and starts to focus.

O'Connor and James duck behind a bush.

O'CONNOR Oh God! A photographer on my first day!

JAMES That's no photographer, that's probably the Committee!

O'CONNOR But she seems to be alone!

JAMES There are one-man committees! They're the *most* dangerous.

Two nurses, Sue and Ellen, are at the wheel of a car which squeals dangerously around a corner and hits

Micha from the left hand side. Micha falls across the hood and slips off in front of the car which crunches to a halt. The nurses are screaming hysterically.

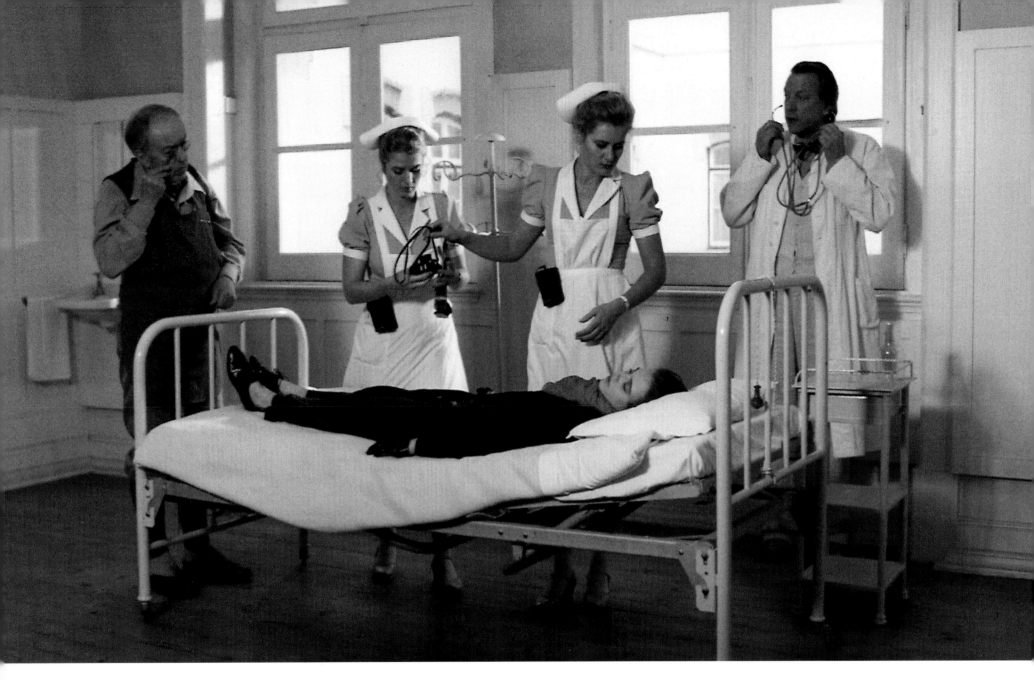

O'CONNOR Are you crazy? Look what you've done!
ELLEN She just threw herself in front of the car!
O'CONNOR Bullshit! I saw the way you were driving. James, get the stretcher!

ELLEN Is she all right? Is she hurt badly? She's so small we could carry her in for you.
O'CONNOR No, no, no. Let's do this properly.
JAMES Oh, Lordy. Can't we get rid of her?
O'CONNOR Of course not! Put her in No. 27.

O'CONNOR'S OFFICE.
O'CONNOR And you were planning to start work here today as nurses?
ELLEN That's right. As temporary nurses.

James is standing under the window with a spade ready to dig a grave in the flower bed. Next to him is Dr. Jacoby's body. James lowers the spade at O'Connor's silent gesture that the flower bed is *not* the best spot for a grave.

O'CONNOR I think that you should plant that somewhere else, James ... James is our gardener. The previous administrative staff of this residential home have just been relieved of their responsibilities and it is up to me to review the commitments that they have made and to see whether or not we will be able to fulfill them. What kind of pay were they offering you?

ELLEN Six hundred and fifty dollars.

O'CONNOR Six...

SUE That's for both of us. For the whole day. Together, it's a bargain!

O'CONNOR Six hundred and fifty dollars a day is an awful lot of money. How long have you been nursing?

ELLEN We do it part-time.

O'CONNOR What do you do the other part of the time?

ELLEN A little show business. Sue does some dancing and I'd like to get into the movies.

SUE We'd both like to get into the movies.

O'CONNOR Show business is quite expensive. I... I think I could probably get nurses who are just nurses ... cheaper, what do you think?

ELLEN Well, you might get cheaper ones, but

you'd run a terrible risk.

O'CONNOR That's a very honest answer. Well, welcome to Nirvana House!

The telephone rings. O'Connor takes the receiver and hands it to James, who accepts it nervously.

O'CONNOR James! I said to plant that somewhere else!

JAMES (on the 'phone) Hello! Louis? Hi! Santa Barbara Hongkong Cafe? Yes, we did call. Yes, this is Nirvana House. We want eight orders of Chinese food... Yes, just eight. Please hurry... we're desperate. Thank you.

OFFICE. O'Connor is showing the new nurses the hospital files

O'CONNOR (leafing through the files) These are

the patients who will be under your care. This is
Mr. Warlock.
ELLEN He's nice!
SUE Which one of us gets him?
O'CONNOR Either one of you, actually. He likes

to get into bed with people.
SUE/ELLEN I know that type...
O'CONNOR No, no, no, he's not that type ... and
this is Mrs. Tannenbaum.
SUE Oh, I've seen her somewhere before.

ELLEN How old is she?
O'CONNOR Well, that's a delicate issue. She
doesn't age. She's been forty ever since I've been
here. We even have trouble convincing her
about yesterday.

SUE/ELLEN (laughing) Oh, that's *your* photo, Doctor!

O'Connor slams his own file shut.

O'CONNOR That's why the previous administration had to be replaced. The files were in total chaos. This is Mrs. Daniels. She, of all our patients here, has the most serious medical problems. She has psychosomatic paralysis of the medulla oblongata and a suspected luxation of the paletta. Are either of you familiar with that kind of condition?

ELLEN It certainly sounds very interesting, but what about that girl upstairs?

O'CONNOR She was run over by a car, wasn't she?

SERAFINA'S ROOM.
SERAFINA My skin is as smooth as a butterfly's wing and the powder lies over it like fine golden dust. But … when the wing is torn, the blood will flow… Oh, unlike you, my butterflies, I am too full of bile and putrefying juices. Aah, Errore!

GARDEN. A young man arrives.
JAMES Who are you?

JOE Hi.
JAMES Are you the young man from Los Angeles? The one for Mrs. Tannenbaum?

JOE L.A., right. But who is Mrs. Tannenbaum?
JAMES I see. Are you American?
JOE No, not really.

JAMES Oh, that's probably better anyway... There is a resemblance. But the moustache has got to go.

JOE What do you mean? Why?
JAMES There's no time to argue. We've got a lot to organise today. Whatever Mrs. Tannenbaum

wants, Mrs. Tannenbaum gets.
SERAFINA'S WINDOW.
SERAFINA Sleep on, don't wake me because I

languish here in the desert! In your glory I shall deck the air with jewels, and you shall fill the sky forever!

GARDEN.
JOE What's that supposed to mean?
JAMES Don't worry about it. She's O.K. I've known her for a number of years. Listen, you'll make a couple of hundred bucks at least.
JOE How long will this take?

JAMES Just follow me.
MICHA'S ROOM. Ellen discovers Warlock applying pollen to the brow of the sleeping Micha.

ELLEN Did you do that? You should leave her alone, you know. She could be concussed.

MR. WARLOCK Not anymore ... pollen of the myrtle flower. When it surrounds the brow, it awakens consciousness.

ELLEN Are you a doctor too?

MR. WARLOCK No ... I saw you arrive from my balcony and I said to myself, "There must be a party over there." I love a little company after lunch. It can get so cold ... Maybe you'd like to

get into bed too? You can get into mine if you like ... No. 24. Down the corridor.

ELLEN Are you looking for trouble, Mr Warlock?

MR. WARLOCK I've been here as long as I can

remember and neither I nor anyone else has ever gotten into trouble... Time to get back to work! Nice meeting you, Miss...

ELEVATOR IN THE MAIN HALL.

DIANA DANIELS I've just seen two nurse's caps.
O'CONNOR That is correct, my dear.

DIANA DANIELS Where are they? It's time for my walk.
MR. WARLOCK She's sleeping, O'Connor.
DIANA DANIELS Who?
MR. WARLOCK She looks like an angel, so exquisitely defenceless.

DIANA DANIELS: Who? Who?
O'CONNOR Nirvana House has a new patient, my dear.

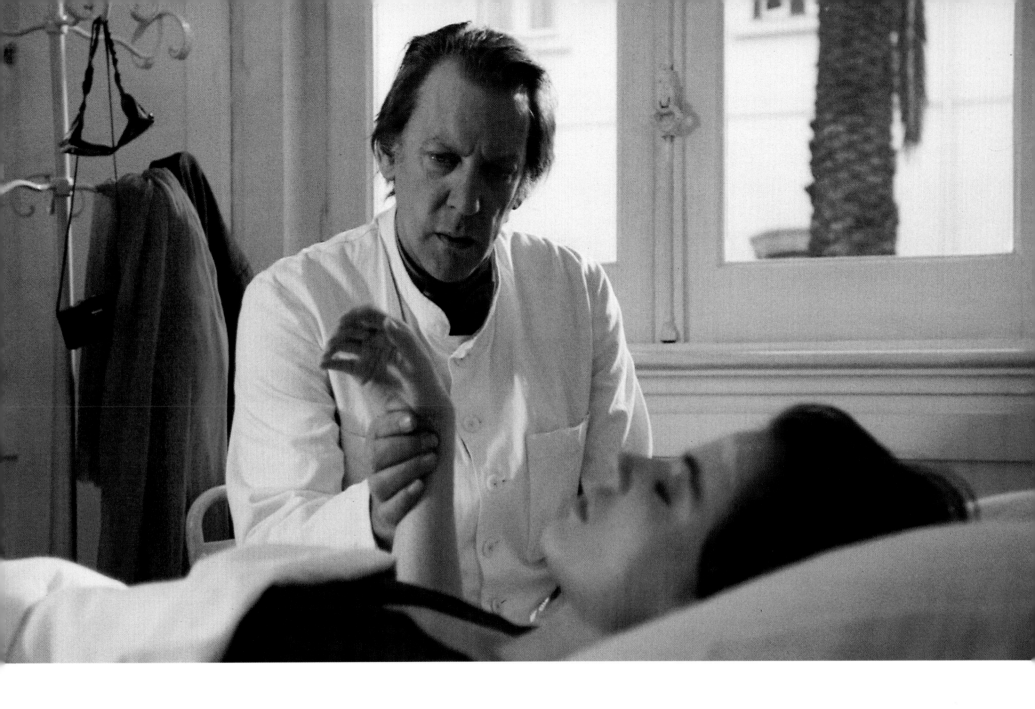

MICHA'S ROOM. O'Connor is observing the new patient. He feels her pulse.
O'CONNOR ... And I will slow it down.   And I will slow it down.   And I will slow it down.

Sue, Ellen and James tap dance in the corridor. MUSIC.
JAMES Ladies! Ladies! Please return to the pool-
side!
GARDEN. Sue and Ellen accompany Mrs. Daniels

through the garden.
DIANA DANIELS Well, he told me to wait for
him at the Loyalty Islands and he'd sail his boat
down there. So I settled into a hotel right next to

the harbor for a couple of years and waited. And
waited. Suddenly it became all too clear that it
was the wrong island.
ELLEN I don't believe it.

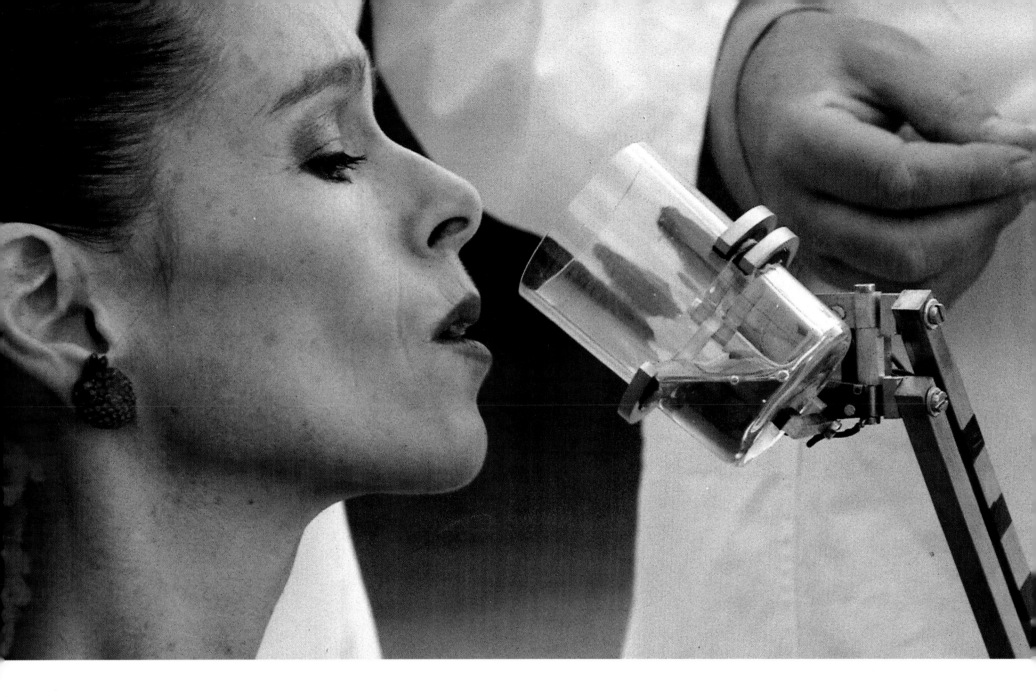

DIANA DANIELS Over a period of time, I gradually lost the use of both my legs. I'm still trying to regain my equilibrium.
ELLEN When they looked at your legs, what did

the doctors say was the matter?
DIANA DANIELS Oh, they said that it was incurable, and I lost interest after that.
O'Connor strides around the pool carrying a bottle

of whisky under his arm.
SUE This is whisky?
O'CONNOR Mrs. Daniels runs for twenty four hours on half a gallon. Now in the future, you'll

be able to handle this procedure on your own.

DIANA DANIELS It's going to be no better here than it was before!

O'CONNOR How can you possibly say that, Diana? These young women are extraordinarily conscientious and you know that for me you are the project of a lifetime.

DIANA DANIELS Don't speak about me as if I'm some kind of obligation! Remember who you are!

O'CONNOR Diana!

DIANA DANIELS O'Connor! O'Connor! It's ridi-

culous to think of that young girl as a patient. She is the representative of the Winterbottom Foundation. She can never be one of us!

O'CONNOR No, of course, never. However she would be an interesting addition.

DIANA DANIELS Even if she would be consi-dered to be a patient of yours, how do you know that she has the willpower? After all, she's been unconscious for hours!

O'CONNOR Yes. *She's been unconscious for hours …*
that's it, Diana. That's it. Precisely!
DIANA DANIELS Binoculars!

MICHA'S ROOM.
MR. WARLOCK There is no point in ringing. They trust us here. We never get up to mischief.

I've been here at Nirvana House as long as I can remember and neither I nor anybody else has ever gotten into trouble.

MICHA I'm in Nirvana House? Tell me, Mr....
MR. WARLOCK Warlock.
MICHA Warlock? ... Mr. Warlock, I'm Micha

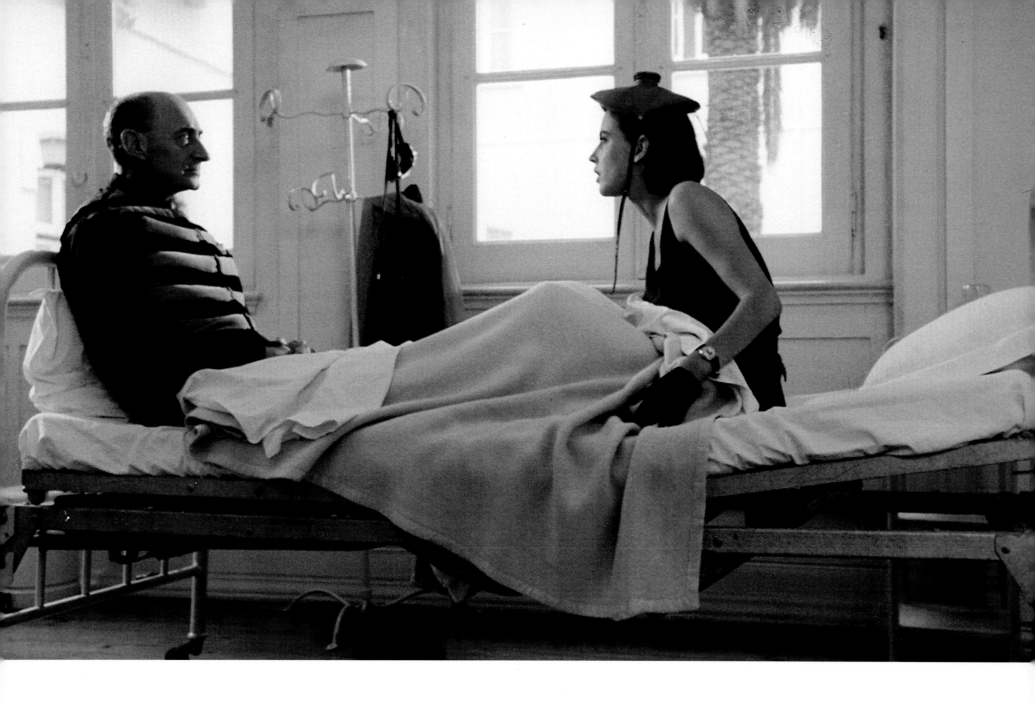

Morgan.

MR. WARLOCK Micha. What a wonderful name!

MICHA Think so, Mr. Warlock? As you've been here so long, you might remember a patient who was here only for a short time, in the year…

MR. WARLOCK No numbers! No numbers!

MICHA Do you have such a terrible memory for numbers?

MR. WARLOCK On the contrary, I have a fantastic memory for them. Fantastic ... absolutely legendary! Every time I hear a number, I can never ever forget it. That part of my brain is stuffed chock-a-block. Ad infinitum!

MICHA What about faces?

MR. WARLOCK Faces?

MICHA You're full of faces, too?

MR. WARLOCK It's not so bad with faces.

MICHA Do you remember a rather small man, sad eyes, straight nose and a thin made-up mouth, who never smiled?

MR. WARLOCK I know who you mean. I know exactly! I can see him right in front of me. Jonathan Stark, the funeral director. He never smiled because nobody ever dies here ... ever ... Do I

not look well?

MICHA Mr. Warlock, you seem in excellent health. But unfortunately you've got the wrong man.

MR. WARLOCK Ask me some more! Ask me some more!

MICHA This man is called...

MR. WARLOCK Oh, no names! No names!

MICHA You're full of names, too?
MR. WARLOCK Different problem. You see, if you say a name and I say no, that's the end of that.

No more conversation. Tragic!
MICHA How will I ever find out if you knew about Buster Keaton?

MR. WARLOCK You're going to have to be clever, aren't you? Isolate the subject.

SERAFINA'S ROOM.
SERAFINA Put your hands on the table. Like that. Yes. Keaton! Where are you? Give us a sign!

Yes, just a little one. Piccolo, piccolo! Oh no, not you, Giorgio. Get on...
Suddenly a little silver fork rises rom the table and

begins to pirouette between Micha and Serafina.
SERAFINA That's him... that's Keaton!
MUSIC.

BY THE POOL.

O'CONNOR Ah! I expect it's the shock. You feel cool.

MICHA No, I feel fine, thank you.

O'CONNOR No, definitely not... I've been watching you. You've been unconscious for nearly three hours. I'm Dr. O'Connor, head physician.

MICHA I'm Micha Morgan, your patient, I suppose.

O'CONNOR Yes, I'm going to confine you to this wheelchair for a while. Relaxation is the appro-

priate therapy under these circumstances. The motto of our foundation is "Relax yourself so that we won't have to relax you!" But, of course, you know that. Take Diana Daniels, for example. When she relaxes herself, she is perfection. Not a muscle moves. Except, of course, if it's a matter of life or death.

MICHA Diana Daniels? The famous swimmer! What is she doing in a wheel chair?

O'CONNOR Conserving her energy.

O'Connor wheels Micha towards Mrs. Daniels.

MICHA Mrs. Daniels, you were just wonderful as

"The Mermaid of Manhattan!" I will never forget your dive through the fire into the Hudson. It was incredible.

DIANA DANIELS How mean of you to bring that up. That particular stunt, young lady, ruined my life.

MICHA Oh, that's terrible! I knew nothing about your accident.

DIANA DANIELS My accident? Oh no, don't be

ridiculous. It wasn't an accident! Professionals don't have accidents! It was a tragedy! That ring of fire, the incredible heat and far below, all

those little boats filled with reporters, tiny as ants. I was frightened to death. I couldn't jump.

MICHA So, it wasn't you?

DIANA DANIELS My agent advised me to take to a wheelchair. I had to get out of my contract. And so, over a period of time, I gradually lost the

use of both my legs... At least it saved me from going bankrupt.

MICHA So you were crippled by insurance. That's an interesting case! If you wouldn't mind, I would like to write about it.

DIANA DANIELS You're going to take notes? (Towards O'Connor) See?

O'Connor disappears with Micha into the garden.

O'CONNOR After the invention of the talkies, a lot of people in the movies went crazy. It's not so surprising when you think about it. Whole floods of them came from the studios to be treated at this institution. Everyone who becomes involved in film voluntarily is endangered.

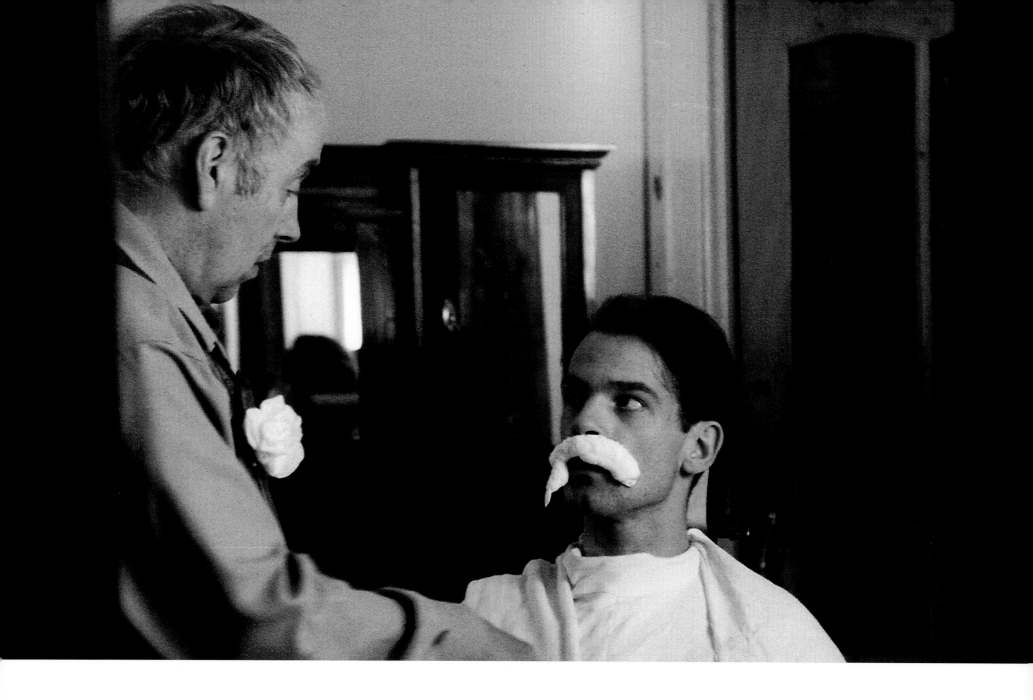

BARBER'S SHOP. James stands in front of Joe, twirling a shaving brush around in a bowl of soap lather. Joe appears as the victim of some sacrificial rite. With one stroke, James covers Joe's moustache.
He takes a step backwards, pulls out a razor from his back pocket and, in one supremely confident ges-

ture, shaves the moustache off with a single sweep of the blade.
Shocked, Joe grabs his upper lip. James takes the photograph from his apron comparing it to the now-cleanshaven Joe. He seems satisfied.

SERAFINA'S ROOM.
SERAFINA I love your hardness, your brutality, Maurice. Although I'm still uncertain. There was one small hope, the hope that I would find you again … Ahh … And then Maurice…
JAMES That's you!

JOE Does is have to be "Maurice?"
SERAFINA Is that all you have to say? ... Oh, Doctor!
O'CONNOR Serafina!

O'Connor, about to perform his first task as a doctor, steps into the room, warily holding a syringe. Serafina sighs and holds out her arm for the injection and looks challengingly at Joe. Joe looks away.

O'Connor is bothered by a passing butterfly which lands behind Serafina's head. At the last moment, he changes his mind and instead pierces the butterfly with the needle and hurries from the room. The but-

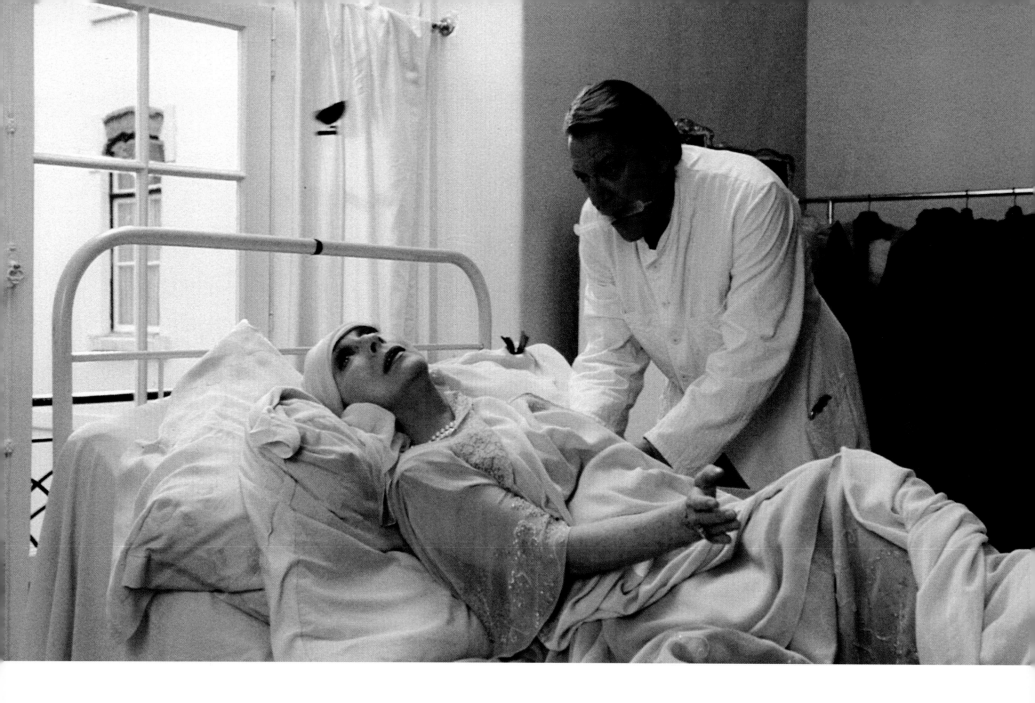

terfly flutters in agony.
Serafina, unaware of O'Connor's action, looks at Joe from the corner of her eye.

SERAFINA The name means nothing to me. It

doesn't even suit you.

O'CONNOR'S OFFICE:

ELLEN Excuse us, Dr. O'Connor, but Mr. Silver is impossible and Mr. Warlock is also very difficult.

He refuses to take his pills at the prescribed times.

O'CONNOR Why?

ELLEN He claims that it should be more random.

O'CONNOR Random? Was that his exact word?

ELLEN No, he used the word "indeterminate."
O'CONNOR In future, Ellen, it would help me in my work if you could be precise.
SUE Mrs. Daniels is also in a difficult mood. She wants me to remove my uniform next time I come.

O'CONNOR Ah, Miss Miller, your uniform not only serves an hygenic purpose, but it is also a symbolic separation between yourself and the patient, and we must never forgo that at any cost.
SUE But then how can I comply with the patient's wishes?

O'CONNOR Keep your cap on! And Mrs. Tannenbaum?
ELLEN Oh, Mrs. Tannenbaum is very happy. Her 'fridge has been fixed.
O'CONNOR Well, as long as Mrs. Tannenbaum has her young man here, you two can take care

of Miss Morgan in her wheelchair.

ELLEN Sue, you can take care of Miss Morgan and I'll take care of the wheelchair.

LENNY SILVER'S ROOM.

LENNY SILVER You see, it's just a matter of finding exactly the right tone. And, what some of the greatest pianists have not realized is that, basically, the piano is not an instrument that is suitable for playing. And there is a world of difference between pianistic vision and pianistic practice, if you get my meaning. Now, with the resources I have at my disposal here, I can hardly hope to eradicate totally such a dichotomy. I could, of course, eliminate the most general of tones, but why bother? I sometimes think it would be better if there were no piano at all. But little by little it has something to do with music.

MICHA I would love it if you would play something more for me.

LENNY SILVER Could you come back next week? I can only work for ten minutes a day. I can't bear anymore. And in between there's only one thing I need and that's relaxation!

MICHA So then, you and Dr. O'Connor understand each other perfectly!

LENNY SILVER Really? Sometimes I think I am

the only one who understands what real work is.
MICHA Oh no, you're wrong! Look at me, I'm a
cinematologist!

LENNY SILVER Stop! I hate film! It was my worst
experience! I wrote a grand score for those
idiots!

MICHA What did they do to you? I know what
they did to...
LENNY SILVER Get out!

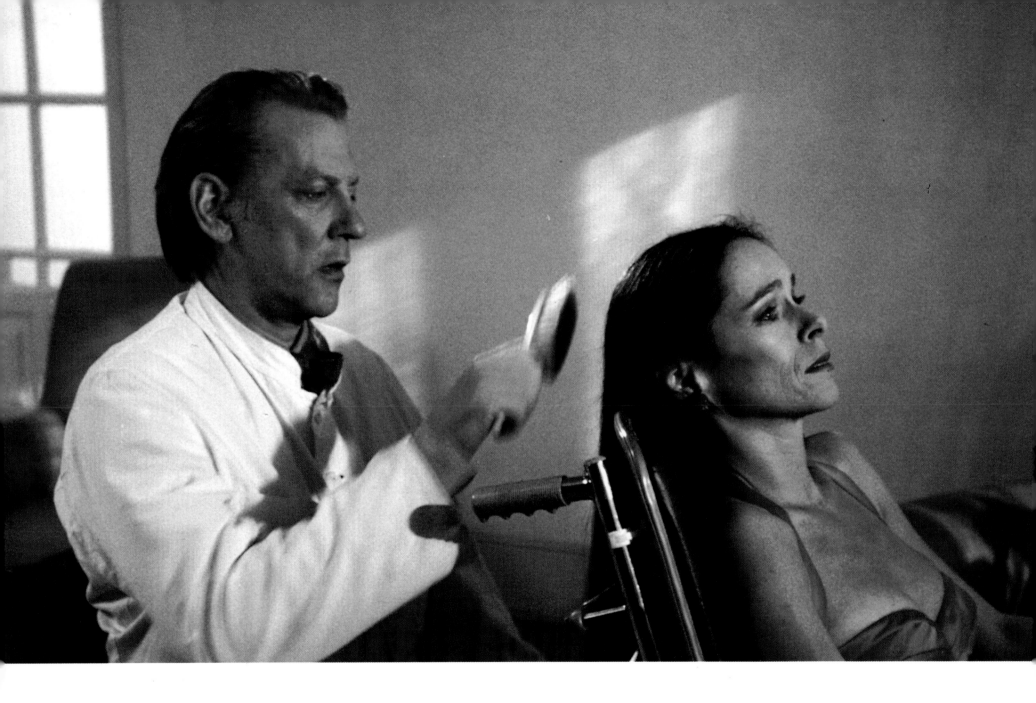

DIANA DANIELS' ROOM.

O'CONNOR You feel like a volcano inside today, Diana.

DIANA DANIELS Bullshit, O'Connor! Bullshit!

I've been feeling so unsettled ever since that little snoop wormed her way in here. She's going to ruin our work.

O'CONNOR It's very important, for all of us here

at Nirvana House, that she feels comfortable, Diana.

DIANA DANIELS Yes, but not too comfortable! If a member of the Ethics Committee suddenly

decides to settle in here, it's going to complicate things rather!

O'CONNOR Not if she's my patient.

DIANA DANIELS But she can't be your patient!

O'CONNOR Why not?

DIANA DANIELS She's spiritually immature! The young have no power of concentration. She'd be absolutely hopeless at immobility training.

O'CONNOR I don't think so.

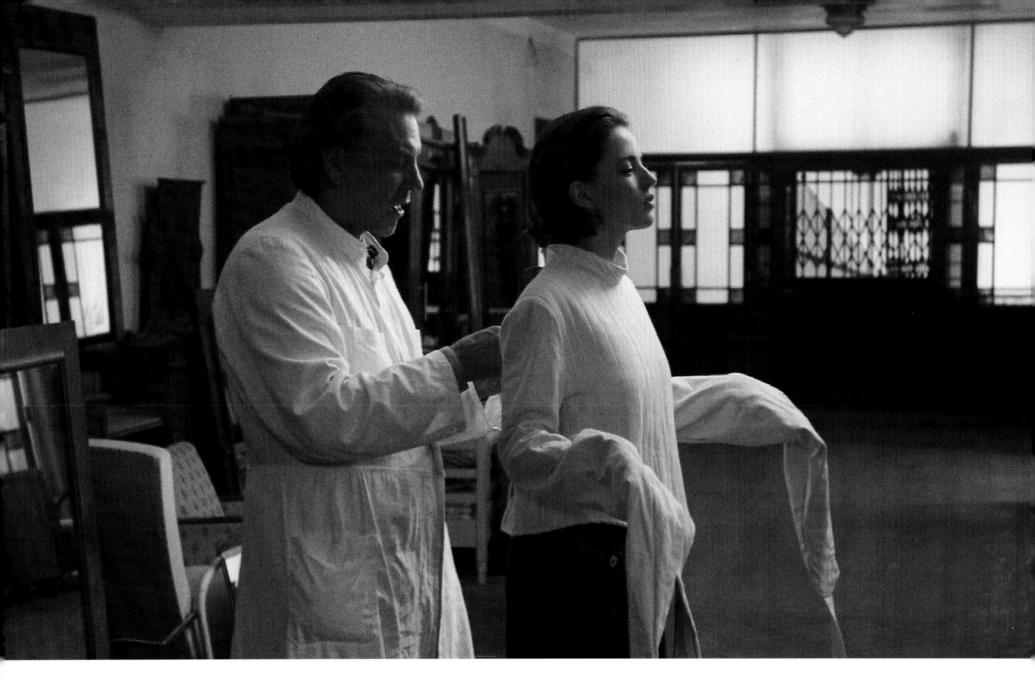

DIANA DANIELS Well then, why don't you just put the young lady to the test?

O'CONNOR What test?

DIANA DANIELS Your special method for parti-cularly stubborn cases!

O'CONNOR That's brilliant, Diana! Absolutely brilliant. What a wonderful way to observe her!

CORRIDOR OF MIRRORS.

O'CONNOR Hello Miss Morgan. I wanted to talk to you about some of the work that we're doing here at Nirvana House. I suppose that you are

probably not aware that some of the greatest revelations in scientific research occur when you take the most mundane concept and turn it inside-out, upside-down. Take restraint, for example. You probably think of restraint as a loss of freedom. But if you take that notion and turn it inside-out, upside-down, restraint can liberate you. This is a ... a straitjacket that we use in our immobility training. Here try ... try it on for just a second. ... quite attractive, isn't it? It looks like one of those old Prussian officer's uniforms.

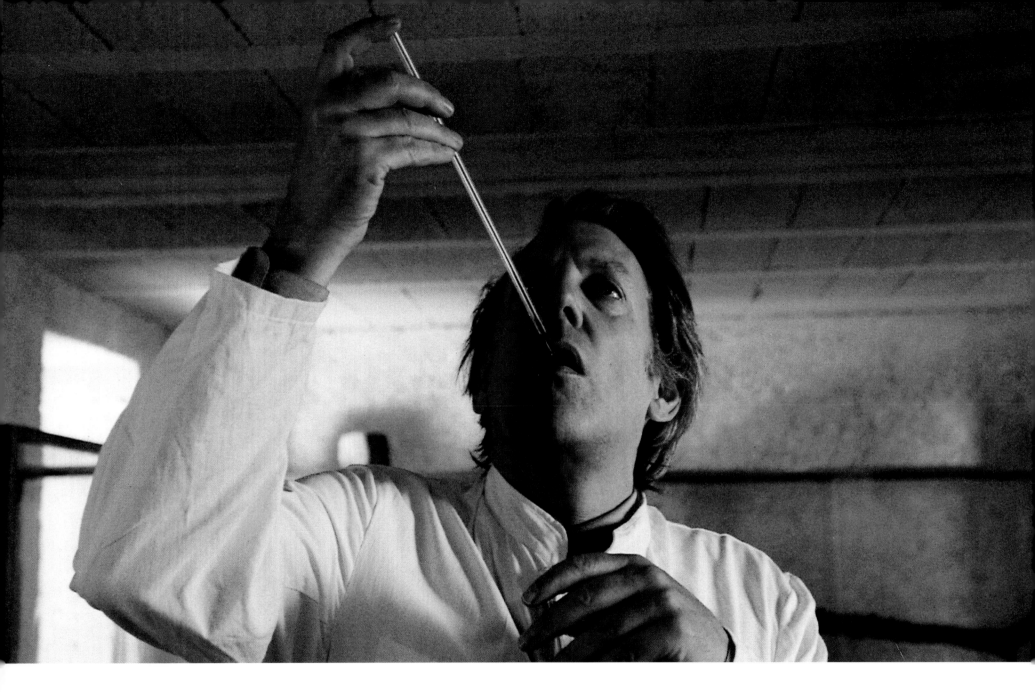

The theory behind it all is that you can use this to keep yourself very still, then you can learn how to gather all your body's energy together at one point so that you are a force so powerful that you'll be able to fly.

MICHA What are you doing, Dr. O'Connor?

O'CONNOR Aren't you interested in my research?

MICHA Yes, but this hurts!

O'CONNOR Then keep still! Don't move! I want you to be comfortable. Don't panic. I want you to get used to this.

MICHA Get this off me!
O'CONNOR Just leave it one, Miss Morgan, just leave it on. You're having the normal reaction of the newly initiated. What you must do, the trick, is to try and relax. Calm yourself down, relax totally within it. Treat it like a second skin.
MICHA You have snake's eyes!
This remark hits O'Connor like an electric shock. He starts to swallow with difficulty. He looks as if he is having some sort of attack. Abruptly, he lets Micha fall to the floor and rushes out into the hallway. Micha is left bewildered and bound up.

ATTIC. Mrs Daniels is watching Mr. Warlock sitting
in his cot, buzzing like a bee, next to the old bathtubs
in the attic of Nirvana House.
Mrs Daniels wheels herself slowly down the corridor

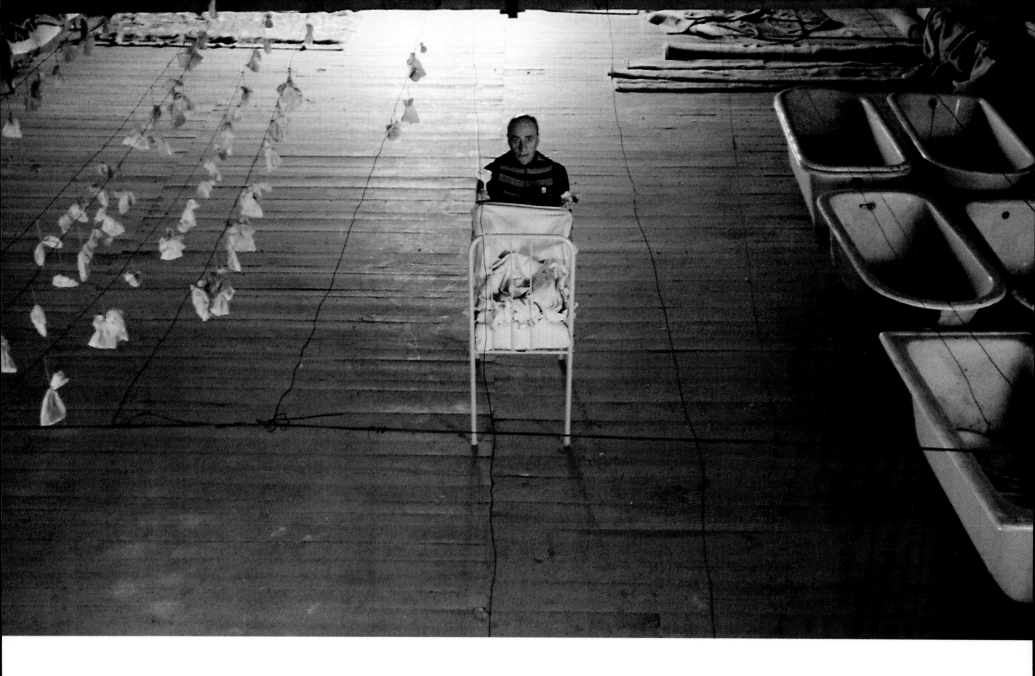

and discovers Micha in the straitjacket at the other
end. Softly, rapidly she propels herself over to her.
For a couple of seconds, tiny flames can be seen fli-
ckering on a wire along the corridor.

EMPTY ROOM.
DIANA DANIELS It suits you, you know.
MICHA He put this on me and then he just went away!
DIANA DANIELS Oh, but that's just Dr. O'Connor. He's like that. There's no use complaining, you know. In this place we have our own code of ethics which says that the doctor is allowed to do exactly as he pleases with us. Listen, you know

once he had me tied up for so long that I lost all desire to move. I mean, even to raise my finger tips.

MICHA Even to fly?
DIANA DANIELS Even to ... It was not a good idea for you to come here, Miss Morgan.

Mrs. Daniels wheels herself towards the door, slamming it behind her. There is no handle on the inside of the door.

Micha is alone in the empty room. Suddenly her body begins to turn slowly; her circling accelerates; she is standing on tiptoe, having transformed herself into a spinning top, propelled by an invisible whip. She becomes a spindle, her feet resembling the tip of a knife. She lifts up off the ground, a white cocoon twirling between floor and ceiling. Suddenly she lets out a short, shrill scream and the straitjacket bursts apart.

All of a sudden Mr. Warlock is there in the room, scrutinizing her.

MR. WARLOCK Unbelievable! What extraordinary impudence! That's *my* straitjacket, Miss Morgan! It is not a secular item and it is not available for your little games!

MICHA I'm sorry, Mr. Warlock!

MR. WARLOCK I'm busy, Miss Morgan!

MICHA Are you planning to be busy for long, Mr. Warlock?

MR. WARLOCK For life!

Mr. Warlock turns with his straitjacket and leaves the room.

SNAKE ROOM.
JAMES Hello, Dr. O'Connor, how are things going today?
O'CONNOR Wonderfully, James. Absolutely wonderfully.
JAMES Stay alert. Miss Morgan is very diligent.
O'CONNOR What do you mean by that?
JAMES She's in the garden, taking photos.
O'CONNOR That's not possible! Someone spoiled everything!

GREENHOUSE.
O'CONNOR Who helped you out of that strait-jacket? Who?
MICHA Nobody! I freed myself.

O'CONNOR You freed yourself? That was a waste of energy. You should have waited for me. You panicked.
MICHA No! I concentrated and then I just burst

out of it.
O'CONNOR That's panic. Panic allows you to realize the body's potential. It's like when you have a motorcycle accident and the motorcycle

lands on you and suddenly you find that you have enough strength to lift it up and throw it off! But the motorcycle is so heavy in reality that you can't even pick it up ... I can teach you how

to relax every muscle in your body ... so that you can gather together all your energy like a conductor with a symphony. That powerful, wonderful explosion of pure force.

MICHA Like Buster Keaton!
O'CONNOR Buster Keaton! Buster Keaton used to live here!
MICHA Did you know him?

O'CONNOR No, that was way before I came here, but I love his movies where he masters danger with that daredevil precision. I mean he *had* it!

MICHA Yes, *so* beautiful.

O'CONNOR Then he lost it. It's so difficult to maintain.

MICHA I wish I had met you sooner. Maybe you could have saved someone I loved. It's too late now!

O'CONNOR Are you sure?

MICHA Yeah, he's gone. I lived with him. He was a composer. He was my father. Do you know what it means to live with a composer? (Micha begins to move rhythmically from side to side) Tick tock tick tock tick tock …

O'CONNOR A metronome! A metronome!

MICHA He made his last work three months ago.

Just before he died in New York. He worked all the time and that metronome was going day and night. I will never forget it. He was such a perfectionist! It's strange, you know … since then I have not been able to get rid of that rhythm. Tick tock tick tock tick tock tick tock. You see,

the first part is easy.
Stiff as a board, Micha lets herself fall towards O'Connor.
O'CONNOR Oh! Are you going to stay here?
MICHA The problem is when I drop forward I don't have the energy to swing back.

O'Connor lifts her gently back to an upright position.
O'CONNOR I can give you that energy. It's no accident that you came here and found me. Do you understand that?

PAVILLON D'AMOUR. Preparations are in progress for Seraphina's performance.

JAMES Now you've got to pretend to be her fiancé, right? You went to join the French Foreign Legion and she comes looking for you in the desert and gets to you just when you're dying.

JOE What do I say?

JAMES Well, you know what happens when people die. Their whole life passes before their eyes.

JOE You want all of it?

JAMES Just the highlights.

Suddenly O'Connor and Micha enter through the aviary.

O'CONNOR It's a wonderful opportunity for you, young man. Just use your own personality,

assuming, of course, that you have a personality of your own.

Joe and Micha look at each other quizzically, at the same time realizing that they have met before. For a moment, the world around them fades away.

JOE Are you... do you belong here?

MICHA Do you think so?

JOE Look at me. I just fit the advertisement.

MICHA Well then, it's just an accident that we meet again.

JAMES The only rival to her beauty that Serafina accepts is you.

MR. WARLOCK Don't be frightened, Maurice, it's only a rehearsal.

JOE If you're talking to me, my name is Joe.

JAMES Serafina has chosen the name Maurice. Of course if you want to live a quite unremarkable life, you can walk out of here and remain plain old Joe.

JOE You're sure there's not going to be any funny business?

Serafina enters the Pavillon d'Amour.

SERAFINA Maurice! Maurice! Oh!

JOE Excuse me?

SERAFINA You're not dead?

JOE Me? No, I'm not dead.

SERAFINA Everyone said you were dead! But you are wounded. Must you die? Must you die now that I have found you again? You feel warm and solid to my touch, not like a dying man. Maurice, I stood at the harbor among thousands of women. We waited for days. I knew you would come, but you did not come. My pain, my

despair was more than I could bear. I'm dying Maurice! Yes, I'm dying! The war was too long and cruel! It's cruelty that kept you young and beautiful. You're such a handsome boy.
JAMES (prompting) You look exactly...
SERAFINA You look exactly the same as before! You haven't changed a bit! You know, I have changed, Maurice. Waiting for so long. James! Bring Maurice a chair! The gentleman is

wounded... are you blind!
Serafina disappears to prepare her next entrée.
JOE What do you want me to do now?

MR. WARLOCK Obey the camera in her mind!
Suddenly, Mrs Daniels wheels in and faces O'Connor.

DIANA DANIELS Where are those two bloody
nurses?
O'CONNOR Since when have you been inte-

rested in Serafina's performance, Diana?
DIANA DANIELS You can't fool me, I knew that girl was here!
O'CONNOR I'm surprised at you, Diana!

DIANA DANIELS Give me a drink!
Serafina dances in pirouettes towards Joe.
SERAFINA To Algiers! To Algiers! To Algiers! And now, Maurice, we are together. Our lives

will be devoted to the holiness of our love. We shall never leave each other again. We shall share every nuance of feeling, our glances shall be fused together.

The nurses enter the pavilion.
SUE/ELLEN Are we interrupting anything?
SERAFINA Oh, you! Figlie di puttane!
JAMES We'll do it again, Mrs. Tannenbaum. Sit

down girls!
SERAFINA So ... we shall never leave each other again! We shall share every nuance of feeling, our glances shall be fused together. Not one

breath of the other shall we miss. We must never slacken our constant vigilance. We must not let fear creep in again.

JAMES (prompting) Such, such a...

SERAFINA Such a what?

JAMES ... tragic flaw!

SERAFINA Of course, I know it very well...Such

a tragic flaw! Let's leave it to the others. And now, Maurice, kiss me! Oh mia vita! Mie sperme! Mie sperme!

Joe's gaze remains fixed desperately on her as she

moves in on him to relinquish herself in one final kiss.

Micha, O'Connor, Silver, Warlock, Mrs. Daniels, James, Sue and Ellen are all utterly engrossed in the

spectacle of Serafina's seemingly never-ending kiss. During the interminable embrace, the others approach and form a circle around the couple. They stare at Serafina whose voluminous costume obs-

cures Joe and the entire rockery.
O'CONNOR (shouting) Cut!
The spell is broken. Joe crawls out from under Serafina, and sees Micha who lifts her tee-shirt for a

second, showing her little tits. She turns and runs away.

SERAFINA'S ROOM.
SERAFINA If you don't feel like it, we needn't stay here. I am free! Yes, I inherited mountains of money from Henry Tannenbaum. The world lies at our feet. Who cares if you want to be Maurice or not? I know how precious one's identity is. I myself hide behind the name of Tannenbaum. And I would never reveal the true name of the woman concealed behind that ridiculous name! Not even to you, Maurice! Not even to you!
JOE I don't want to know either. I like you just as Tannenbaum. You know what? If you really

want to, you can call me Maurice.

SERAFINA That is a great lesson in life: what one gives, one gets in return. When you were not here, I saw you in so many faces. Hundreds of Maurices. But I was deceiving myself. You are the only one, unmistakable, splendid Maurice.

Suddenly the door is thrown open. Micha, impatient, looks into Serafina's room. Joe looks at Micha while Serafina grabs Joe's arm as though to keep him from running away with Micha. A second later, the door slams shut.

JOE Shouldn't we go down and join the party?

SERAFINA Oh yes, my darling!
CORRIDOR. Micha meets James in the corridor.
MICHA Where is Dr. O'Connor! I'm leaving and

I want my bag!
JAMES Dr. O'Connor? Let's find him!
PARTY ROOM.

MR. WARLOCK What a lovely couple!
SERAFINA My dear friends, and all of you with
whom I lived here now so happily and for so

long, rejoice with me! Maurice has returned from the war. From now on we shall never be parted again!

DIANA DANIELS Whisky!

SERAFINA When you are unhappy, dear friends, you need a home and kind people to take care of

you. But when you are happy, you can be any-where in the world! So Maurice and I are going to Paris. We're leaving you to build our own little

nest in France. And when Paris loses its charm, we shall go to Venice. Venezia! City of my birth! By the light of the full moon, Maurice shall swim across the Grand Canal for me! He will blossom golden under my sun!

JAMES Bravo! Bravo! Fabuloso, Mrs. Tannenbaum! I shall visit you. I could do with a change myself.

MR. WARLOCK I shall make a personal appear-

ance in Paris. Armand! Where is Armand?
DIANA DANIELS Where is Dr. O'Connor?
Has anyone see Dr. O'Connor? What is all this

rubbish about Paris? Venice! Grand Canal!
Dr. O'Connor will forbid it. This is all there is.
Have you forgotten your contract?

SERAFINA Cara mia, love knows no barriers!
DIANA DANIELS Whisky!

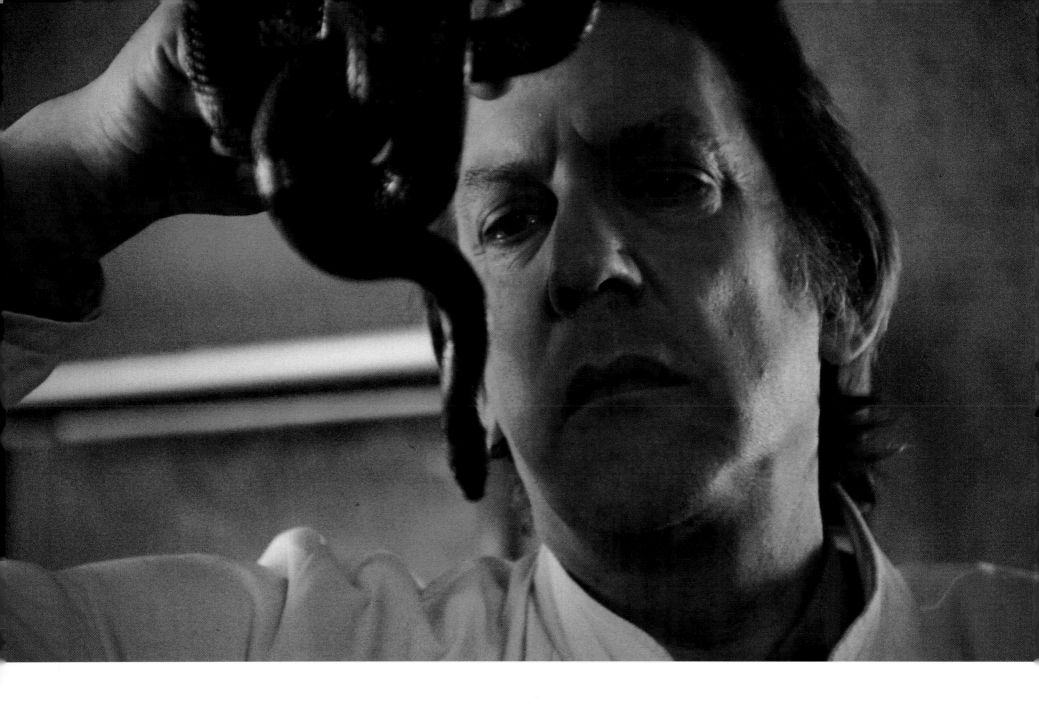

SNAKE ROOM. O'Connor is provoking the snake to strike at a small sponge that he has prepared to absorb its poison. They are both engaged in an hypnotic form of foreplay. The inner tension of O'Connor's body is transmitted to the snake. The rhythm of its tail increases.

Micha quietly enters the room and takes in this fascinating ritual.

She draws closer and suddenly the mutually hypnotic concentration between O'Connor and the snake is broken. As O'Connor turns to look at her, the snake snaps out of its trance and strikes sideways

at Micha, biting her on the arm.
Micha screams. O'Connor jumps up, trying to re-
strain her. Micha pulls out her knife. O'Connor
knocks it out of her hand. He holds her in an iron

grip, pressing her to the floor.
MICHA (screaming) No! Don't you have any anti-
serum?
O'CONNOR No, I really don't have...

He shakes his head wildly, bends over her and bites
her arm. Micha, chalk-white with pain, faints.
O'Connor sucks the snake bite.

Mrs. Daniels opens the elevator door, wheels past the storage rooms and pushes open the door to the courtyard just in time to catch a glimpse of Micha and O'Connor. She stiffens.

Dr. O'Connor holds Micha unconscious in his arms

and dances around with her like a shaman, singing "Me and Bobby McGee."

O'CONNOR Busted flat in Baton Rouge
Waitin' for a train
Feelin' near as faded as my jeans

Bobby thumbed a diesel down
Just before it rained
Rode us all the way to New Orleans
I pulled my harpoon and in my dirty red bandanna

Playin' soft while Bobby sang the blues
Windshield wipers keepin' time
Holdin' Bobby's hand in mine
We sang every song that driver knew
Freedom's just another word for nothing

left to lose
And nothin' honey ain't nothin'
If it ain't free
Exhausted, O'Connor carries Micha back into the
room, sits down with her in an old leather armchair

and stares helplessly into space.
MICHA Am I going to die?
O'CONNOR No. No, no, you're going to live.
There is a song that goes with that snake:

Let my curious tired neck rest with yours
Dance with me if you can.
Sing for me when you bleed as in life or death
Live with me, live.

SERAFINA'S ROOM. Joe wakes up, slips naked out of bed and opens the 'fridge. The yellow light from the 'fridge melds with the blue of the room. Nothing to drink, but hundreds of blue butterflies asleep in the cold interior. Joe looks in amazement and then pushes the door shut again. In an instant he is back in bed and asleep. The door of the 'fridge is worn, It opens again slowly and the light from within paints a yellow triangle on the floor.

MRS. DANIELS' ROOM. Mrs. Daniels is sitting in front of her large mirror. With a shaking hand, she brings the lipstick to her mouth. With agonizing effort, she colors her lips fiery red.

SERAFINA'S ROOM. Slowly the butterflies wake from their cold-induced lethargy. They begin to escape,

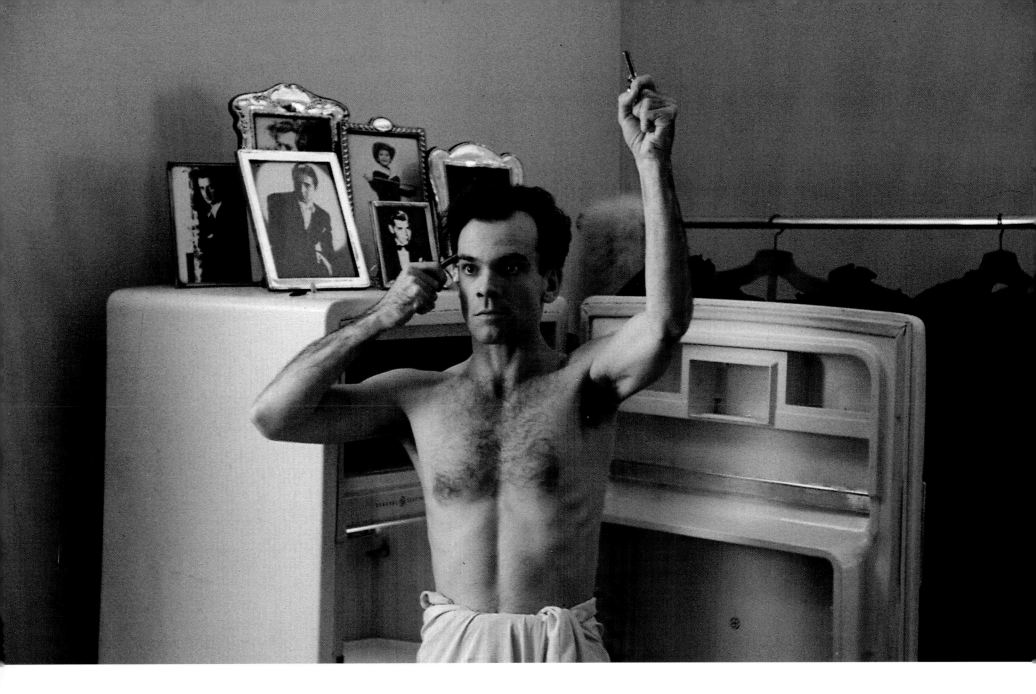

one by one, from the 'fridge, soon emerging in small, vibrating blue clouds. Serafina wakes up
SERAFINA (sighing) Maurice! Maurice! Maurice! The fluttering "souls" are filling the room. Serafina is suffocating in the clouds of butterflies.

SERAFINA My souls have strayed. I cannot find their resting place. In the cool dark of oblivion they waited to fill new bodies ... beautiful vessels! And now, my children will be the spoils of madness!

JOE Serafina! Serafina!
SERAFINA Who are you?
JOE Me? I'm Maurice!
SERAFINA I don't know you! Get out ... You are obscenely alive. You're nothing but a joke next

to the men who have died for my sake. Get out of my sight!

Joe has an inspiration. In a flash he grabs Serafina's pistols.

JOE I'll kill myself if you want!

SERAFINA Yes, do it!

Joe shoots down a butterfly. Shocked, he looks at Serafina. Serafina turns away. Joe smiles victoriously. After a short pause, Serafina turns towards him again and in seconds has metamorphosed into a

totally different person, cold, sober and devoid of any dramatic stance.

SERAFINA Bravo! Well done! Get dressed! Get out! Immediately!

Next morning. THE BASEMENT OF THE SNAKE ROOM. Micha closes the door behind her and almost falls into Mrs. Daniels' lap. She leaps backwards as Mrs. Daniels skillfully manoeuvres her wheelchair, backing Micha into a corner.

DIANA DANIELS Now I know what you have been up to, you little slut!
MICHA It's not what you think!
DIANA DANIELS Oh! It's *not* what I think?
MICHA No, I've been bitten by a snake!

DIANA DANIELS You've been bitten, already? Then show me!
MICHA I've just been through a horrible experience.
DIANA DANIELS And he sucked you too!

MICHA Of course, otherwise I'd be dead now!
DIANA DANIELS Get out of here!
MICHA But Dr. O'Connor said...
Micha steps back with horror. Mrs. Daniels pursues her in her wheelchair. Suddenly, Micha stumbles across the wheelchair containing the dead Dr. Jacoby.
DIANA DANIELS What Dr. O'Connor? Get out of here! Wait! Listen to me. This is Dr. Jacoby who until yesterday was the director of Nirvana House. So you see, your beloved O'Connor has not held his position for quite as long as you seem to think! We're all one soul here! Don't think you can spend your honeymoon with just one of us!

COURTYARD. Micha staggers out of the house, takes a deep breath and leans against a nearby wall.

SERAFINA'S WINDOW. Serafina is struggling to get her large boudoir mirror up on to the window sill.

Finally, she manages to balance it on the edge and, peering into it, cries:

SERAFINA I want to be left alone! Release me from my image!

She gives the mirror a final shove and, exhausted, watches it fall.

COURTYARD. The mirror shatters into a thousand fragments right next to Micha who almost expires

from shock. Just as she regains her composure, a whip cracks over her head.

Micha turns around, horrified, to find Mrs. Daniels poised for action with a large whip. Micha takes to her heels as quickly as she can. Mrs. Daniels, with uncanny speed and agility, pursues her in her wheelchair.

AVIARY. Micha comes running out of the blue door into the pavilion, past an astonished James who has just finished digging a grave in which Dr. Jacoby is now lying. The wheelchair and his shoes are next to

the grave. Mrs. Daniels follows Micha with her whip to the aviary. All the birds fly agitatedly around their cages.

AT THE POOL. The wheelchair, minus Mrs. Daniels, chases Micha down a narrow shrub-lined path towards the pool. In the distance, at the other end of

the pool, a wooden chair does a backward flip and collapses.

Micha, about to collapse herself, turns to avoid the

advancing wheelchair only to find Mrs. Daniels before her, on her feet, the whip held high above her head. Micha has no alternative but to dive into the

pool. She swims away underwater.

Mrs. Daniels reaches back to bring the whip forward with all her strength. At the same moment, the

wheelchair, hurtling out of control, crashes into her back.

She falls into the water and the wheelchair plunges

in after her, smashing against her spine.
Micha reaches the other side of the pool, pulls herself out and runs off as fast as her legs can carry her.

Mrs. Daniels' body slowly sinks beneath the surface
of the water.

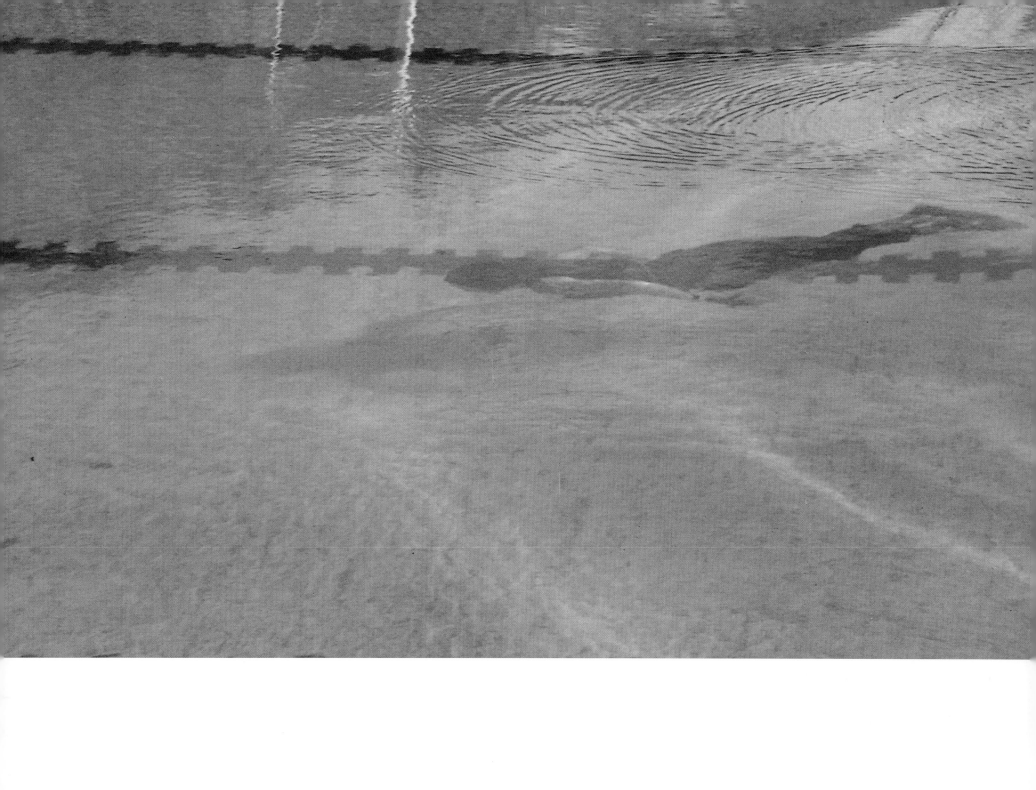

COURTYARD. Sue and Ellen are chasing butterflies.
O'CONNOR Good morning, ladies! What's the matter?
SUE We've been working for hours on the butterfly shift!

ELLEN Mrs. Tannenbaum is very difficult. She refuses to have her breakfast before her entire butterfly crew is back in her 'fridge.
SUE And they're so hard to catch!
ELLEN But we're working on a strategy to tire them out.

O'CONNOR That's what they do in New Caledonia. Have either of you seen Miss Morgan by any chance?
SUE Just a glimpse. She was moving *fast*.

ELLEN And so was Mrs. Daniels! It all looked rather funny to me, come to think of it...
O'CONNOR I'd rather not, actually. Do you know, by any chance, in which direction they were running?

GARDEN. James pushes a distracted Joe to the gate.
JAMES Here's your money, Joe. Why don't you go?
JOE But where is Micha?
JAMES Quien sabe? Who knows?

SWIMMING POOL. All of the inmates of Nirvana House are gathering in a semi-circle by the edge of the swimming pool.
The wheelchair is standing half-submerged in the shallow end. Its arm has begun to move; the glass is collecting water and then pouring it out.

SERAFINA I consider this a betrayal. She was the one who was always so strict about keeping the rules. Her death is desertion!

MR. WARLOCK Death is not provided for at all in our world. If everyone here was allowed to die, then we wouldn't need Nirvana House!

LENNY SILVER Yesterday morning we had no doctor and today we've lost a patient. I must get back to my piano. Let's elect another patient

right away.

O'CONNOR It's not that easy. Mrs. Daniels was ideal. She was the enterprising spirit of Nirvana House, right up until her last breath. I'm going to miss her...

JAMES Oh Lordy, we'll all miss her. Without the right number of patients we're sunk. And don't forget ... the Committee is still around.

The telephone rings. James answers.

JAMES Nirvana House ... Yes ... I understand ...

I understand you correctly ... not here ... not at all? ... Next year? Ah, of course! Naturally! That was the Winterbottom Foundation in Los Angeles. They apologize for having failed to show up yesterday.

O'CONNOR Failed to show up?
JAMES They've postponed their visit until next year. Of course I gave them the impression that everything is running as usual.
O'CONNOR But Miss Morgan...

JAMES I understood from the message that they aren't coming. Thus they can't be here. I believe Miss Morgan hasn't anything to do with the Winterbottom Foundation!
O'CONNOR What an opportunity! If Miss Mor-

gan isn't the Committee then she is free to become my patient!
LENNY SILVER I'm only prepared to tolerate her if she stays out of my room, preferably in her *own* bed.

MR. WARLOCK I've already been in her bed! We played guessing games. She was rather nice...
O'CONNOR Sue, would you have Miss Morgan come to the pool please?

ELLEN Well... that is a difficult one, Dr. O'Connor. Miss Morgan has left!
O'CONNOR What?
JAMES If she has taken her car she won't be

going very far! I took her gas for our ambulance as we need to be ready for all emergencies!
O'CONNOR James, you're outstanding!

AT THE OCEAN. Slowly Micha's car begins to splutter. It comes to a stop. She climbs out, opens the bonnet and attempts to fix the engine.

While she is bent over the hood, she hears the sound of a distant engine. She looks up and sees the old white ambulance from Nirvana House, its red light flashing, and an old Ford approaching from far away.

Micha goes rigid with shock. She attempts to barric-

ade herself in her car when she realizes that the ambulance has pulled up about a hundred yards away from her.

O'Connor climbs out, without taking any notice of her, and opens the back door of the vehicle. Then, very politely, he helps Mrs. Tannenbaum, Lenny

Silver, Mr. Warlock and James out of the ambulance. With the help of Sue and Ellen he lifts Mrs. Daniels' wheelchair out of the back.

Now they all gather in front of the ambulance in a friendly group, very decorative, the wheelchair in the centre.
Micha looks over at them, completely bewildered.

Nobody says a word. Then Dr. O'Connor gives the wheelchair a push. It moves along the road like a well-oiled machine, making a bee-line for Micha. As the wheelchair flashes past her and continues on

its solitary route along the ocean front towards oblivion, everyone from Nirvana House is dancing to wild and crazy rock 'n' roll.

Micha joins O'Connor who swings her around
amongst the patients. We see Micha switching from
one partner to another, making her way impercept
ibly towards the ambulance.

In a moment she is in the ambulance and takes off along the road.
The others are left standing astonished, in a blue cloud of exhaust fumes.

O'Connor realizes that Micha has escaped and runs after the ambulance. He comes menacingly close and grabs the back door by the handle. Suddenly he disappears from the screen.

INSIDE THE AMBULANCE. Micha looks in the rear view mirror and finds that she has lost sight of the group from Nirvana House. Gradually, she relaxes and speeds down the road to the music from the

old record player.
As she makes a sharp turn, something black slides across the floor towards her. She glances quickly down at her feet to find a black snake. Shocked, she

slams on the brakes.
The needle of the record player gets stuck and starts to repeat the same fragment of music.
Micha looks down again and realizes that it is noth-

ing more than a piece of black tube. One of Serafina's big blue butterflies has woken up and flutters excitedly back and forth in front of Micha's face.
Micha's nerves are on edge.

She relaxes as the dance music begins again, then stiffens suddenly and turns around suspiciously. Through the small window of the divider, two eyes are staring at her. Joe and Micha look at each other in astonishment. Micha loses control of the car which speeds up on to a track leading to the ocean and starts to spin out of control. The faces of Micha and Joe relax into a blissful expression.

The ambulance, skidding from side to side, heads for a gigantic billboard on which a large plate of spaghetti is painted. A five-foot, three-dimensional fork is stuck in the middle. The ambulance smashes at full speed into the cement post of the billboard. The fork quivers violently and somersaults to the ground. The ambulance explodes. The fork then stands itself upright and begins to dance in graceful pirouettes up into the sky above the ocean.

MUSIC.

The old Ford of Nirvana House moves quickly down the ocean road stopping near the scene of the accident.

O'Connor, Serafina, Warlock, Silver and James get out. They approach the burning ambulance hesitantly.

O'Connor is the first to turn and walk towards the cliff to stare out to sea. Suddenly, as though he has just discovered something, he takes his binoculars and focuses on the sea. In the distance, he spots Micha and Joe sporting together like little dolphins on the waves.

O'Connor watches them for a while, in a melancholy mood. Then he adjusts the binoculars, putting them *out* of focus, and hands them to Scrafina who gives them to Warlock who gives them to James.

All appear to be looking in a bored fashion at the waves. Only Lenny Silver directs the binoculars towards the sky, just in time to see the last pirouette of the dancing fork.

MUSIC.

O'Connor	DONALD SUTHERLAND
Diana Daniels	GERALDINE CHAPLIN
Serafina Tannenbaum	VALENTINA CORTESE
Micha	AMANDA OOMS
Mr. Warlock	DAVID WARRILOW
James	TAYLOR MEAD
Lenny Silver	ARI SNYDER
Joe	MARTIN WUTTKE
Sue	NINA FRANOSZEK
Ellen	LENA LESSING
Jane	MARY WORONOW
Boyfriend	STEVE OLSON
Mrs. Noah	TILLY LAUENSTEIN
Dr. Jacoby	ABEL FERNANDES
Nurse Fowler	MARIA DULCE
Screenplay	REBECCA HORN
	MARTIN MOSEBACH
Director	REBECCA HORN
Executive Producer	GEORGE REINHART
Producer	LUCIANO GLOOR
Co-Producer	AIMÉE DANIS
Associate Producers	HENRIQUE ESPIRITO SANTO
	MARTIN WIEBEL
Line Producer	UDO HEILAND
Director of Photography	SVEN NYKVIST
Operator	KEVIN JEWISON
Focus Puller	PASCAL MUNDT
Clapper/Loader	SUSANNE PETERSEN
Still Photographers	ALFRED RASCHKE
	MARIANNE FLEITMANN
First Assistant Directors	GABRIELE MATTNER
	SABINE ECKHARD
Script Supervisor	KERSTIN SCHWARZBURG
Sound Mixer	UWE KERSKEN
Boom Operator	JOCHEN HERGERSBERG

Art Director	NANA VON HUGO
Assistant Art Director & Set Dresser	MARTIN SCHREIBER
Set Designer	ANTONIO CASIMIRO
Assistant Set Designer	XANA OLIVEIRA E SANTOS
Property Master	JOAO LUIS
Assistant Property Master	ARMINDO COSTA
Construction Coordinator	CARLOS FERREIRA
Construction Team	ABILIO SOLEDADE
	ALBERTO FERREIRA
	DOMINGOS COSTA
	ANTONIO CARRILHO
	PAULO ARAUJO
Translator	LENA SANTOS
Creative Property Artist	HASJE BOEYEN
Assistant Property Artist	JOS VAN TILBURG
Costume Designer	FRANÇOIS LAPLANTE
Costumes Valentina Cortese	ROBERTO CAPUCCI
	MILA SCHÖN
Wardrobe	JUSCHKA FRIEDEMANN
	CONSTANCE DONATH
Dressmaker	"ALTAZY" – ANGELA BRUNO
Seamstress	LUCILIA OLIVEIRA
Hair & Makeup Artists	BERND-RÜDIGER KNOLL
	MARTINA RASCHKE
	UDO RIEMER
Makeup Donald Sutherland	ANN BRODIE
Gaffer	ULRICH LOTZE
Electricians	DIRK VOSSMERBÄUMER
	RALF 'KALLE' DOBRICK
Key Grip	TREVOR WATKINS
Generator Driver	HORST KUTZELMANN
Special Effects	HARRY WIESSENHAAN
Special Effects Assistant	EDUARD WIESSENHAAN

Stunts	ISABEL SANTOS
	ELPIDIO FERREIRA
Animal Trainers	CARLO GUIDI
	MIKE CULLING
	MARC RICHMAN
	ROGER WARREN
	ANTONIO BISPO
Choreography	LISA LICCINI
	ARMANDO JORGE
	KIMBERLEY RIBEIRO
Production Manager	MIGUEL CARDOSO
Location Manager	GÜNTER FENNER
Production Coordinators	CHRISTIANE STEIN
	SILVIA ROCHA
Production Secretary	FILOMENA RODRIGUES
Assistant to the Producer	MONIKA FAEH
Assistant to the Director	CAROLINE BOURGEOIS
Drivers	ANDRE TRINDADE
	JOSÉ LUIS PERES
	NENE COSTA
	ANTONIO ROCHA
	CARLOS BATISTA
	ANTONIO JOSÉ
Legal Advisor	JANET JACOBSON
Auditor	KAL-KÜHL GMBH
	FRITZ PETER LÜTYENS
Accountant	LUIS 'BIBI' HORTA
Catering	MANUEL CERVEIRA
	JOSÉ SOUTO
	ANTONIO FLORIDO

BERLIN UNIT

Assistant Property Master	JÖRG BRUNS
Construction Team	CLAUSING & WREDE
Drivers	LENA REUTER
	FRANK OBERÜBER
Catering	PETRA ROSPERT
Post-Production Manager	CLAUDIA CHRISTEN
Editor	BARBARA VON WEITERSHAUSEN
Sound Editor	GISELA LÜPKE
Assistant Editors	OLIVER GIETH
	CARLA BOGALHEIRO
Trainee Editor	SANDRA SCHMIDT
Music composed by	SERGEY KURYOKHIN
Musicians	POST-SOVIET ANIMAL GROUP
	"POP MECHANICA"
Piano and Electronics	'WOLF' SERGEY KURYOKHIN
Guitar	'GOAT' ALEXANDER LYAPIN
Bass	'OWL' ALEXANDER TITOV
Trumpet	'COCKROACH'
	VYACHESLAV GAYVORONSKY
Saxophone	'ELEPHANT' MICHAEL KOSTIUSHKIN
"Diana-Song" composed by	INGFRIED HOFFMANN
Musicians	PETER BAUCHWITZ-TRIO
Foley Artists	JOERN POETZL
	THOROLF DORMA
Re-Recording Mixer	MARTIN STEYER
Visual Effects	FUTUREFFECTS BERLIN
	FRANK SCHLEGEL
Titles Design	META DESIGN
	ULI MAYER
Opticals	THOMAS WILK
Color Consultant	DETLEF FLEISCHHAUER

LOS ANGELES UNIT

Unit Production Managers	REZA MIZBANI
	GABRIELA BACHER
Clapper/Loader	PETER IOVINO
Electrician	RAINER STONUS
Key Grip	BRIAN VILLEGAS
Sound Assistant	JAMES BENNET
Makeup/Hair	MIMI LESSEOS
Stunt Coordinator	TERRY JAMES
Stunts	MARIA KELLY
	RAWN HUTCHINSON
	JAY COX
Production Assistants	FRANÇOISE GRANDJEAN
	JAMIE JENNINGS
	DAVID MAX
Catering	MARY'S GOURMET CATERING

Special thanks to:

PONTUS HULTEN

JANNIS KOUNELLIS

ERIC FRANCK

TIMOTHY BAUM

PETER RAUE

CLARE DOWNS

GERMANO CELANT

IDA GIANELLI

KAREN AMIEL

SAM FRANCIS

ERIC ORR

BUSTER'S BEDROOM is a German-Canadian-Portuguese Co-Production of
METROPOLIS FILMPRODUKTION GMBH & CO KG, BERLIN
LES PRODUCTIONS DU VERSEAU, MONTRÉAL
and PROLE FILM LDA., LISBON

in association with

LIMBO FILM AG, ZÜRICH
and WESTDEUTSCHER RUNDFUNK, KÖLN

with the participation of

SENATE OF THE CITY OF BERLIN
TÉLÉFILM CANADA
SOCIÉTÉ GÉNÉRALE DES INDUSTRIES CULTURELLES-QUÉBEC